BLACK COUNTRY
STEAM
WESTERN REGION OPERATIONS
1948–1967

BLACK COUNTRY
STEAM
WESTERN REGION OPERATIONS
1948–1967

PAUL DORNEY

PEN & SWORD
TRANSPORT

AN IMPRINT OF PEN & SWORD BOOKS LTD.
YORKSHIRE – PHILADELPHIA

First published in Great Britain in 2022 by
Pen and Sword Transport
An imprint of
Pen & Sword Books Ltd.
Yorkshire - Philadelphia

ISBN 978 1 39909 032 2

A CIP catalogue record for this book is available from the British Library.

Typeset in 11/13 Palatino by SJmagic DESIGN SERVICES, India.

Printed and bound in India by Replika Press Pvt. Ltd.

Pen & Sword Books Ltd incorporates the imprints of Pen & Sword Books Archaeology, Atlas, Aviation,
Battleground, Discovery, Family History, History, Maritime, Military, Naval, Politics, Railways, Select, Transport,
True Crime, Fiction, Frontline Books, Leo Cooper, Praetorian Press, Seaforth Publishing, Wharncliffe and White
Owl.

For a complete list of Pen & Sword titles please contact

PEN & SWORD BOOKS LIMITED
47 Church Street, Barnsley, South Yorkshire, S70 2AS, England
E-mail: enquiries@pen-and-sword.co.uk
Website: www.pen-and-sword.co.uk

or

PEN AND SWORD BOOKS
1950 Lawrence Rd, Havertown, PA 19083, USA
E-mail: Uspen-and-sword@casematepublishers.com
Website: www.penandswordbooks.com

CONTENTS

INTRODUCTION

'The Black Country' is the term applied to a small area of north-west Worcestershire and south-east Staffordshire, to the west of the city of Birmingham. Any use of the name invariably gives rise to dispute as to its precise boundaries, but purists would maintain that it can only be applied to that area where large deposits of local coal and limestone gave rise to widespread iron production and the development of associated industries. I am mindful that by this definition Wolverhampton and Stourbridge probably should be excluded, the city of Birmingham certainly should. Nevertheless these places are, in the railway context, too significant to omit, and I beg licence to include them in the pages that follow.

In the early years of Black Country industrial development a network of canals provided the means of transport for materials and manufactures, but railway promoters were eager to tap into this lucrative traffic and quickly put forward appropriate schemes. Many of the lines in what some may call the 'true' Black Country ultimately fell into the hands of the Great Western Railway and its Northern Division, based on Wolverhampton. These lines later formed part of the Western Region of British Railways and, despite transfer to the London Midland Region in 1963, retained most of their 'Western' character until the end of local steam in early 1967.

My own interest originated when, at the age of about seven, I accompanied my older brother to the local railway station to watch the passing trains as a way of amusing ourselves during the school summer holiday. His interest soon waned and passed to other things, but I was captivated. In due course further visits there led to my meeting like-minded individuals and together we formed friendships that have continued until the present day. Without their assistance and encouragement the compilation of this book would not have been possible. The book is presented merely as a photographic record of the trains and landscape of the area rather than offering a history of the lines covered. Fine historical records have been published elsewhere and should be consulted by those whose appetites have been whetted. Where possible hitherto unpublished photographs have been used, although in some cases it has been necessary to sacrifice a little quality in order to include material of such interest as to warrant inclusion.

Throughout the 1950s the area's railways flourished, with a diversity of locomotive types and traffic unrivalled in much of the country. It is not the same today. The Black Country landscape of the 1950s and early 1960s has changed dramatically since the photographs in this book were taken. The three large steelworks have closed, as has much of the heavy industry which gave the district its name. Their sites are now occupied by large housing developments, retail parks, or road improvement schemes. Most of the lines featured in the book have closed. The West Midland line has closed completely north of Round Oak and most traces of it obliterated from Dudley to Priestfield. Wolverhampton Low Level has closed and the line on which expresses from Paddington once thundered on their way to Birkenhead now sees nothing but suburban trams. Even the majestic Birmingham Snow Hill station now operates as a mean subterranean station beneath an office block. At the time of writing only two locations generate any goods traffic; a steel distribution depot based at the site of Round Oak Steelworks receives regular loads of steel coil from South Wales, and a scrapyard at Handsworth sends occasional loads for export. Only the line from Stourbridge to Snow Hill remains to offer a conventional rail journey. Whether these changes are beneficial the reader alone must determine, but I hope this book goes a small way to redress the photographic neglect of the local railway network, and rekindles a few happy memories.

Paul Dorney
2021

1. Blowers Green Junction was the local station which provided my initiation into the delights of railways. In this 1964 view pannier tank 8718 takes the main line with an up trip working, or Bank Train as they were known on the Western Region, bound for Stourbridge Yard. The Windmill End branch is seen in the foreground, controlled by the junction signal box, a standard Great Western design. The station booking office stands at the end of New Road bridge, whilst the whole scene is dominated by the commanding presence of Dudley Town Gasworks. The other notable local landmark, 'Top Church', properly the Parish Church of Saint Thomas, can be seen on the skyline. *(Richard Taylor)*

ACKNOWLEDGEMENTS

The compilation of this book would not have been possible without the assistance offered by others, who generously provided both information and illustrations. My particular thanks go to my old friends from 'Blowers', John Harris, Richard Taylor, Lawrence Brownhill and Brian Lowe, who put me straight on factual matters and provided many photographs, and to Peter Green who encouraged me initially to undertake the book and was of great help in preparing the photographs for publication. I am grateful also to Simon Dewey who was extremely helpful with regard to matters involving Wolverhampton, to Paul Burchill, who searched through his own photographic collection and furnished useful material, to Keith Hodgkins who liaised with David Wilson and Terry Hyde to secure their generous contributions and to David Waldren, who raided his extensive photographic collection at my request to provide elusive images. I am indebted to Andy Williams, who kindly prepared a map to assist those unfamiliar with the local geography. I must also thank Lawrence Waters of the Great Western Trust at Didcot for his assistance in making available to me the photographs of the late Michael Hale, without which the book would have been much poorer. The identities of all photographers are given where known. In instances otherwise photographs are taken from negatives held in individual collections and are attributed accordingly.

MAP OF THE LINES FEATURED IN THIS VOLUME

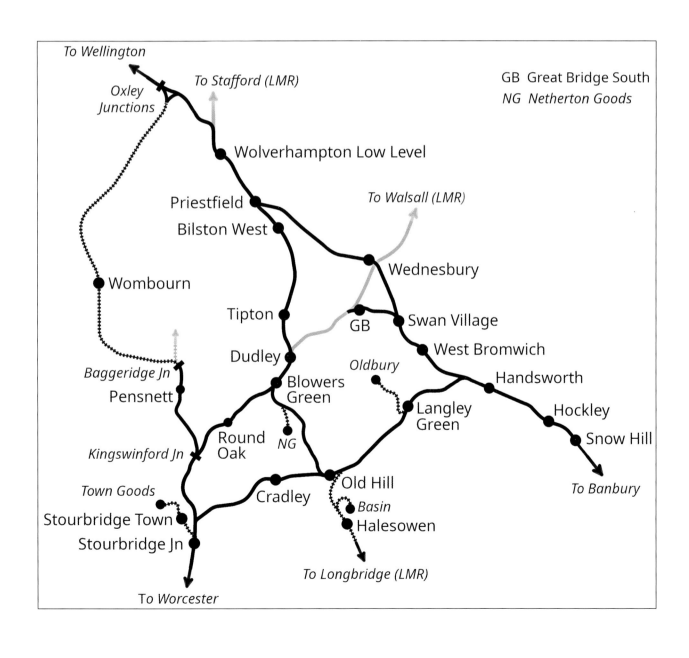

To Wellington

Oxley Junctions

To Stafford (LMR)

GB Great Bridge South
NG Netherton Goods

Wolverhampton Low Level

Priestfield

Bilston West

To Walsall (LMR)

Wombourn

Wednesbury

Tipton

GB

Swan Village

Dudley

Oldbury

West Bromwich

Baggeridge Jn

Blowers Green

Handsworth

Pensnett

Langley Green

Hockley

Round Oak

NG

Snow Hill

Kingswinford Jn

Town Goods

Old Hill

To Banbury

Cradley

Basin

Stourbridge Town

Halesowen

Stourbridge Jn

To Longbridge (LMR)

To Worcester

THE WEST MIDLAND LINE

The West Midland line through the Black Country was the final section of the Oxford, Worcester and Wolverhampton (OWW) Railway. The OWW was the promotion of Black Country businessmen dissatisfied with the service offered by the monopolistic London & Birmingham Railway, and who sought an alternative in the form of a separate line to the south providing transport for their merchandise. Originally backed by the Great Western Railway, the promoters were aggrieved when the terms of the GWR's financial agreement were altered due to a national financial crisis and they broke with the GWR, concluding an illegal agreement with the London & North Western and Midland companies to work the line. A 'gauge struggle' ensued, with the OWW company having an obligation to lay broad gauge track, but a reluctance to do so. Mixed gauge track was eventually laid in this section on the down line only, but only one broad gauge train is ever recorded as having run, and that by way of test with borrowed stock. The OWW was forced by Parliament to complete the section from Priestfield to Wolverhampton against its wishes. Wolverhampton was reached in 1854, shortly before the completion of the Birmingham, Wolverhampton and Dudley scheme, which had been identified by the Great Western board as providing the better route for its main line to the north. When the OWW, which gained the soubriquet 'Old Worse and Worse' for the state of its operations and finances, was finally taken over in 1863 by the Great Western Railway as part of the West Midland Railway Company, it was thus condemned to play its role as a secondary route, far removed from the ambitious ideas of its original promoters.

STOURBRIDGE

2. The southern approach to Stourbridge Junction lies through a long sandstone cutting which extends much of the way to the next station, Hagley. The 8.0 am Birmingham-Cardiff is seen leaving the station behind Hereford's 6989 *Wightwick Hall* in the early 1950s. *(Keith Tilbrook)*

3. Stafford Road's 5010 *Restormel Castle* passes the South signal box with the 9.35 am Worcester-Crewe, having taken almost one hour to cover the twenty-two miles from Worcester. It will take almost a further hour for the twelve miles to Wolverhampton, stopping at all stations en route. A 5101 class tank gets ready to follow into Platform 2 with a Birmingham line service once the 'Castle' vacates it. *(Keith Tilbrook)*

4. The 5101 class tanks were the mainstay of local suburban services until the advent of diesel units. Longstanding Kidderminster engine 5110 is seen entering the station with the 12.40 pm Birmingham-Bewdley local on 10 September 1949. *(Henry Casserley)*

5. In view of our title it is appropriate to include a locomotive of local manufacture. A number of the 1896 Wolverhampton-built '655' class survived into nationalisation, including 2712 seen here in the up sidings on 24 January 1948. It was withdrawn in 1950. *(David Waldren Collection)*

6. It was still possible in the 1950s to travel from Wolverhampton to Paddington via the West Midland route. The 8.14 am Wolverhampton-Oxford prepares to depart behind 5088 *Llanthony Abbey*, in around 1954. Locally-based tank 5151 stands on what was termed 'the Middle Road'. *(Author's Collection)*

7. An unidentified working is seen in the up main platform with a very presentable 5032 *Usk Castle* in the mid-1950s. The 'Town Car' providing connection to the Town station can be seen in the platform to the far left while an insulated Palethorpe's sausage van awaits collection from the Middle Road. Such vehicles were often to be seen at Stourbridge, as Palethorpe's premises were situated at Dudley Port. *(Keith Tilbrook)*

8. Auto trains served not only the Town station, but also other routes. Here Stafford Road's 6418 is seen approaching the Junction station with a working from Wolverhampton on 10 September 1949. *(Henry Casserley)*

9. A Snow Hill-Hereford train slows for its booked stop with Hereford shed's 4905 *Barton Hall*. Hereford and Tyseley sheds shared the majority of these workings at this time, 1954. *(Keith Tilbrook)*

10. A West Midland line local from Wolverhampton threads the lines at Stourbridge Middle Signal Box to gain the relief platform behind 4960 *Pyle Hall* of Reading shed in around 1955. A goods train is leaving the down yard and steam rising above the coaches indicates another goods in the No.1 loop. *(Keith Tilbrook)*

The Stourbridge Town and Goods Yard Branch opened for traffic in late 1879. Its course from the Junction station changed after the Junction station's resiting in 1901. Thereafter the branch left in a north-westerly direction on a steeply falling gradient, double track as far as the Town station and single thereafter. In 1935 the Town signal box was closed and the branch was operated as two distinct single lines, one terminating at the Town station the other proceeding to Amblecote Goods Yard and canal transhipment shed.

11. The service between Junction and Town stations operated to connect with main line services and generally took the form of an auto-fitted tank locomotive and a single trailer car which would operate over fifty journeys each way every weekday. It is seen here at the Town station with two trailers and 1414. An Iron Mink van is stationed beyond as a rudimentary buffer stop. The right hand track proceeds to the Goods Yard. *(Keith Tilbrook)*

12. Stourbridge's 1414 stands in the Town station after arrival from the Junction with the 'Town Car' in around 1955. To the left can be seen the local Midland Red bus terminus. *(Keith Tilbrook)*

13. Beyond the Town station the gradient steepened to 1 in 27 for the final section to the Goods Yard. Runaways were a constant danger, particularly as the line ended at buffer stops which abutted the town's High Street. For that reason the pictured Angel Street Stop Board required all traffic, including light engines, to stop before proceeding down the incline. *(Keith Tilbrook)*

14. The Goods Yard finally closed in September 1965. It is seen here shortly after closure. Beyond the building a private siding of Bradley & Co., protected by crossing gates, crossed the Lower High Street. *(Paul Dorney)*

15. Such was the severity of the climb from the yard that loadings were strictly limited. Here 5754 makes good progress up the incline with the afternoon No.3 Bank Train to the Junction yards. The covered wagons probably contain locally-quarried foundry sand, an important source of traffic for the Town Yard. Stourbridge's engine shed can be seen on the skyline. *(Keith Tilbrook)*

Above: **16.** The up sidings at the Junction station were used for stabling coaching stock. Shrewsbury's 2244 is seen in around 1956 with what will probably form the afternoon Severn Valley working from Kidderminster. *(Keith Tilbrook)*

Opposite above: **17.** A Birmingham-Worcester service approaches behind 8105, one of the 1938 rebuilds of the 3100 class with higher boiler pressure and slightly smaller wheels. Kidderminster's 4596 awaits in the No.1 up loop with a pannier tank visible beyond. Note the old pattern 5' signal arms, which will soon be replaced by the more modern BR(W) variant. *(Keith Tilbrook)*

Opposite below: **18.** There were always some trains which passed non-stop through Stourbridge Junction without visiting the yards. One such was the 11.0 am Crewe-Bristol Class 'C' goods, seen going well through the station behind 6934 *Beachamwell Hall*. A large number of pigeon baskets awaits collection from the up platform, whilst a diesel multiple unit has replaced the 5101 tanks on the Birmingham line service. The diesel units came into general use on that line in 1958. 24 October 1964. *(Paul Dorney)*

Above: **19.** The 1.30 pm Cardiff-Birmingham Snow Hill heads north away from the station behind Tyseley's 7913 *Little Wyrley Hall* in around 1955. *(Keith Tilbrook)*

Opposite above: **20.** The layout of the junction at Stourbridge North Signal Box at that time is shown to good effect as 6950 *Kingsthorpe Hall,* surprisingly running without safety valve cover, passes with an afternoon Wolverhampton-Worcester local. The coal merchant in the up yard appears to have completed his day's work. *(Keith Tilbrook)*

Opposite below: **21.** A young trainspotter looks on as 5022 *Wigmore Castle* passes the North signal box with the midday Wolverhampton-Paddington service at some time during the early 1950s. The Extension line to Old Hill and Birmingham curves away to the right. *(Keith Tilbrook)*

22. Stourbridge's 6393 is seen with a special working from Cardington (Beds), taking Royal Air Force National Service recruits to their training camp at RAF Bridgnorth on the Severn Valley line to Shrewsbury. The Mogul would have probably taken over the train in an engine change at Dudley. c1958. *(Keith Tilbrook)*

23. Bank Holidays would bring a different type of special working, with excursions from the industrial Midlands towns to places such as Stourport and Bewdley. After six miles of falling gradient Walsall shed's 44078 has steam to spare as it approaches the junction. It will be a different story on the homeward return. The London Midland Region authorities seem determined to squeeze another revenue-earning trip from that aged clerestory coach. c1952. *(Keith Tilbrook)*

24. The midday Wolverhampton-Paddington approaches Stourbridge with 4000 *North Star*. Additional carriages would be added at Worcester. The winding gear visible on the skyline of Peter's Hill was in conjunction with local fireclay workings, an important industry in the area. c1953. *(Keith Tilbrook)*

25. To the north of the junction stands Stambermill viaduct, a ten arch blue-brick structure built in 1882 to replace an earlier timber version. The piers of the original can be seen clearly in this picture of 5008 *Raglan Castle* crossing with a Wolverhampton-Worcester train in the mid-1950s. The locomotive shed is evident to the left. *(Keith Tilbrook)*

26. Access to the engine shed was afforded by Stourbridge Engine Shed Signal Box. Here Worcester's 5914 *Ripon Hall* is seen with an up West Midland local passing locally shedded 5658 held in the up goods loop, where unfitted goods trains would stop to pick up brakes pinned down at Round Oak. Another locomotive appears to be moving off shed. *(Keith Tilbrook)*

27. Stourbridge engine shed, originally built as a four-road straight shed, was replaced in 1928 by a standard Churchward design roundhouse, the last of its type to be built. The old shed was retained, initially for railcars, but additional war traffic led to its being used once more for the servicing of steam locomotives. Newport's 7241 is seen outside the old shed in around 1948. Railcars of the two differing styles can be seen within. *(Author's Collection)*

28. A general view of the shed yard in 1964 with local resident 6842 *Nunhold Grange*. An 8F stands outside the repair shop. *(Author's Collection)*

29. At the rear of the roundhouse could be found the sand furnace, where 6679 is seen stabled between duties on No.14 road. Pannier tank 4665 and visiting 8F 48685 are just visible within. 17 January 1965. *(Paul Dorney)*

30. On one of the turntable roads is seen 7414, one of a type retained principally for Halesowen branch work. Upon closure of the Halesowen-Longbridge line in 1964 Stourbridge's remaining allocation of these locomotives was withdrawn en masse. 1963. *(Author's Collection)*

31. The shortest of the twenty-eight turntable roads were used for the stabling of the shed's many pannier tanks. Three of those still in service are seen during their weekend break from work in the last months of the shed's operation. 20 March 1966. *(Paul Burchill)*

32. The end of 1964 resulted in a number of Stourbridge withdrawals, amongst which were the last two working Great Western Moguls, 6364 and 6395, the latter of which is seen here on the former coal stacking road with two other casualties, 6137 and 4153. 17 January 1965. *(Paul Dorney)*

33. With plenty of ammunition to hand the local adolescents seem to have taken it out on the roundhouse windows, as visiting Oxley based 44919, apparently cleaned for special duties, stands alongside the shed. 1964. *(Author's Collection)*

34. Stourbridge's Repair Shop attended not only to the resident fleet and passing failures but, if required, to locomotives sent for repair by neighbouring sheds. Here Oxley's 6870 *Bodicote Grange* appears to be receiving attention to its crank axle or bearings. Note the two stationary boilers used to generate power for the shop's machinery. *(Author's Collection)*

35. Longstanding Kidderminster resident 8718 is seen on accommodation wheelsets whilst the axleboxes and bearings are attended to. On Kidderminster shed's closure in September 1964 this locomotive and its fellows there would be transferred to Stourbridge. *(Author's Collection)*

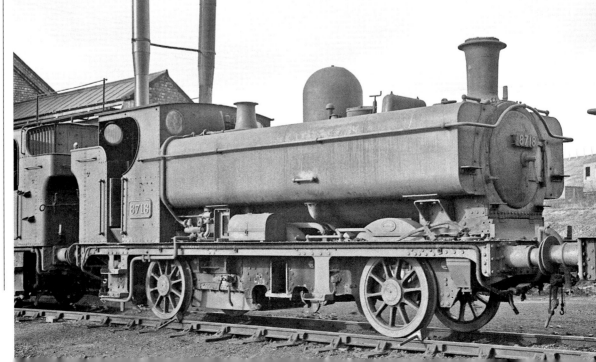

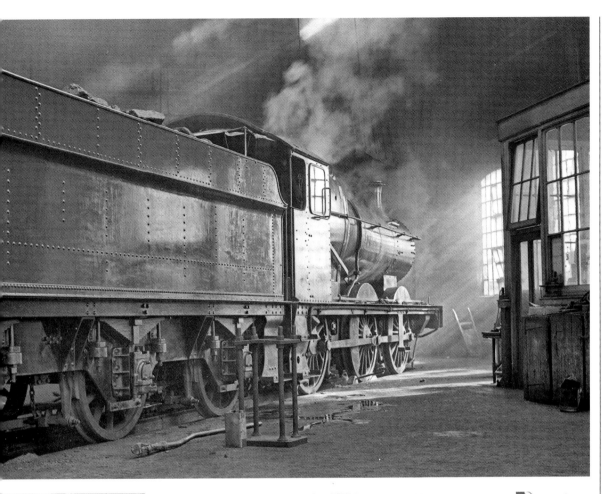

36 & 37. The last steam visitor to the shed was Collett 3205, privately purchased for use on the nascent Severn Valley Railway. It is seen inside the roundhouse, alongside the mechanical foreman's office undergoing a steam test, and at the by then disused coal stage. February 1967. *(Paul Dorney)*

ASSISTING ENGINES

Traffic on both lines north from Stourbridge faced difficult gradients which warranted assistance. Usually four locomotives from the shed would be rostered daily exclusively for banking duties. Banking locomotives would assist in the rear heavy goods trains to Blowers Green on the West Midland line, and to Rowley Regis on the Extension line towards Birmingham. They would also operate in both directions on the 'Bumble Hole', as the Windmill End Branch was known.

38. A type of locomotive which saw regular use for banking was the 5101 Class tank. Here 4151 is seen trailing the 6.35 pm Bilston-Banbury ore empties on the 'Bumble Hole'. The hard work will start after Cox's Lane crossing. This locomotive was a late arrival at Stourbridge and was withdrawn within weeks, a few days after suffering collision damage in April 1964. *(Richard Taylor)*

39. A number of additional Stanier 8Fs were allocated to Stourbridge in the mid-1960s, having been displaced from elsewhere, and were also used for banking, along with the classes of smaller tank engines. 48550, transferred to Stourbridge from Willesden, is seen lending a helping hand through Brierley Hill station. March 1966. *(Paul Dorney)*

40. The summit on the West Midland line was just short of Dudley Tunnel. Bankers would assist from Stourbridge uncoupled, halt at the tunnel mouth, and use the crossover to the up main preparatory to undertaking their next duty. Banker 6692 is seen falling away after banking 8109 with a down Bordesley-Dudley goods. April 1964. *(Paul Dorney)*

41. Passenger trains which exceeded the permitted loadings were piloted by an assisting locomotive, as seen here at Stourbridge Junction North. A 'Hall' takes a heavy excursion train round the sharp curve on to the Extension line, piloted by locally based 5199. Having a leading pony truck, the 5101 tanks were preferred to the 56XX for piloting work. *(Keith Tilbrook)*

STOURBRIDGE-WOLVERHAMPTON

42. The Black Country landscape is shown to good effect in this view of Stourbridge's 6683 struggling through Brettell Lane station with a down goods in around 1961. The neighbouring firebrick works in Meeting Lane appears to be in full production. *(Peter Reeves)*

Above: 43. A Wolverhampton-Stourbridge auto-train awaits departure from Brettell Lane. 6418 has been mockingly decorated by the shed staff at Stafford Road, which provided the locomotives for these workings until they ceased in 1962. A selection of parcels awaits collection by the next down train. Stations such as Brettell Lane and Brierley Hill were retained for parcels traffic after closure of the line to passenger services. *(Peter Reeves)*

Opposite above: 44. One of the many local Bank Trains, probably No.2 from Princes End, proceeds steadily down the bank through Brettell Lane behind 3658. The siding on the left served Harris and Pearson, manufacturers of retort firebricks, used in Gas Works for the production of town gas. *(Peter Reeves)*

Opposite below: 45. Kingswinford Junction South Signal Box controlled the junction for the Wombourn Branch, which can be seen leaving to the left, and extensive sidings serving local industries, including to the right, the glassworks of Stevens & Williams (Royal Brierley) and the abattoir of meat processors Marsh & Baxter. The scene is captured during a period of work to stabilise the cutting side, with an unidentified 56XX in attendance. *(Peter Reeves)*

Above: 46. Stourbridge's 9614 has arrived from Pensnett on No.18 Bank Train with a rake of foreign vans and is signalled into the headshunt at the box, prior to propelling its train into the yard in the dying days of local steam operations in March 1966. It was near this point that there occurred in August 1858 what was described by the investigating officer of the Board of Trade as 'decidedly the worst railway accident that has ever occurred in this country'. A coupling broke on an excursion train as it stopped in Round Oak station, and the runaway carriages collided with a following train. Fourteen lives were lost. *(Paul Dorney)*

Opposite above: 47. A short Wolverhampton-Great Malvern pigeon train ran daily throughout the summer months. It is seen here passing under Moor Street bridge after leaving Brierley Hill behind 73020 of Weymouth shed with a single Gresley-designed brake. The locomotive would have arrived at Wolverhampton on a Saturdays-only service from Weymouth and be retained for use by Oxley shed until its return the following Saturday. 17 August 1965. *(Paul Dorney)*

Opposite below: 48. Viewed from Moor Street bridge, the 6.5 pm Wolverhampton-Stourbridge local leaves Brierley Hill behind Stafford Road's 3778. Visible behind the train is Kingswinford Junction North Signal Box. 1962. *(Peter Reeves)*

49. Two northbound light engines, 7435 and 3658, are seen having passed Brierley Hill station which can be seen in the distance. The short spur from the up line, seen to the left, was used for the despatch of Marsh & Baxter Ltd's meat products from its local factory. *(Peter Reeves)*

50. The 3.20 pm Wolverhampton-Stourbridge Parcels, including the customary Palethorpe's sausage van, drifts past the sports ground between Round Oak and Brierley Hill stations behind 7818 *Granville Manor* on 20 May 1964. After laying over at Stourbridge Junction the engine and stock will form the 4.55 pm to Worcester, the next leg of the Palethorpe van's journey to South Wales. *(Richard Taylor)*

51 & 52. The 3.0 am Pontypool Road-Oxley Sidings, consisting entirely of wagons of coal, labours towards Round Oak behind 3826, banked in the rear by Stourbridge's 9614. *(Peter Reeves)*

Above: **53.** A down local with Shrewsbury shed's 6380 in charge slows to a halt in Round Oak station to pick up its two passengers. An impressive selection of posters decorate the waiting room wall to tempt passengers with the prospect of a summer holiday in the sun. 1962. *(Peter Reeves)*

Opposite above: **54.** Round Oak was dominated by the local steelworks, previously known as the Earl of Dudley's Steelworks. It boasted a large internal railway system, part of the Pensnett Railway, which extended to Dudley (Dibdale), Baggeridge, Ashwood Canal Basin, and to Cradley on the Stourbridge Extension line. The motive power in the 1950s was provided by a fleet of some twenty Andrew Barclay 0-4-0 and 0-6-0 saddle tanks, an example of which, *Lady Honor* (AB1998 of 1933), is seen outside the Wallows Engine Shed. Behind is one of the replacement diesels, No.0 (RSH6979). The steelworks staff uncharitably claimed that the No.0 was an accurate appraisal of its usefulness. *(Author's Collection)*

Opposite below: **55.** In later years the Steelworks produced steel only from scrap. Despite this the proprietors saw fit only twice to buy redundant BR locomotives for cutting up. The first group, of locomotives withdrawn by the Western Region in 1960, comprised 2278, 2284, 2811, 4201, 4217, 5356, 5393, 5788, 7769, 7797, and 5818, seen here preparatory to scrapping. *(Thomas Bassindale)*

56. The second batch, which arrived in 1964, consisted entirely of groups of redundant Eastern Region 2-8-0s from Langwith Junction, with one locomotive in steam dragging its fellows to their fate. An elderly O4 63577 is seen in the Works yard awaiting its turn for the cutter's torch. March 1964. *(Richard Taylor)*

57. The steelworks can be seen in the distance in this view from Round Oak North Signal Box as 44829 approaches with the 10.35 pm Tavistock Junction-Crewe 'C' class goods. To the left can be seen Lord Ward's Canal. 1965. *(John Harris)*

58. Parkhead Viaduct was another OWW structure rebuilt in brick from one with wood supports, this time around 1878. It carried the railway over the Birmingham Canal and its branches, between Round Oak North (Woodside) and Blowers Green Sidings. The return Great Malvern pigeon empties train is seen crossing behind Oxley-based 7806 *Cockington Manor*. 1964. *(Richard Taylor)*

59. After enjoying a day at Dudley Zoo the passengers on a day excursion from Moreton in Marsh make their way home past Blowers Green Sidings behind Worcester's 7920 *Coney Hall* on 18 May 1964. Whilst the excursionists admired the animals and the Norman Castle the 'Hall' would have run down to Stourbridge shed for turning and servicing. *(Richard Taylor)*

Above: **60.** Blowers Green Sidings are seen at both sides of the main line as 8F 48460, banked in the rear, struggles the last yards towards the summit with a transfer freight for Bescot yard. A pannier tank attends to the up yard, where there was a connection to the small internal railway system of Grazebrook's. This firm ran two Peckett locomotives in operations between the yard and their Netherton Iron Works situated adjacent to those of John Thompson, seen on Cinder Bank above the rear of the train. 1964. *(John Harris)*

Opposite above: **61.** A loaded Cardiff-Soho Pool oil train apparently makes light of the climb past Blowers Green Junction Signal Box with ex-works 48700, but the banking 56XX is doing its fair share of the work. Behind the box can be seen the premises of the South Staffs Wagon Co. which generated much of the traffic in the sidings. 29 May 1965. *(Paul Dorney)*

Opposite below: **62.** The Windmill End Branch can be seen diverging right as 4173 takes the main line, returning to Stourbridge with what is probably No.2 Bank Train from Bilston and Princes End. *(John Harris)*

63. Local workers make their way home from Blowers Green station as the 5.29 pm Wolverhampton-Worcester draws to a halt with Oxley's 6839 *Hewell Grange*. The young trainspotters have stayed on to see whether the 5.29 pm produced anything unusual, but will go home disappointed. *(Peter Reeves)*

64. The station closed in 1962 and was demolished shortly afterwards, the results of which can be seen as 2859 passes with the 3.0 am Pontypool Road-Oxley on 20 May 1964. This locomotive was the last to be outshopped by Wolverhampton's Stafford Road Works before closure, a few weeks prior to the date of this photograph. *(Paul Dorney)*

65. The 10.26 am Bordesley Junction-Dudley has arrived at Blowers Green from the Windmill End Branch in order to detach wagons for repair at the wagon works. Train engine 6633 of Tyseley shed has shut off for the stop, but banking sister engine 6678 carries on enthusiastically. 29 June 1964. *(Paul Dorney)*

66. Transfer freights between the London Midland Region and the Western Region were a regular feature of the section of the line between Dudley and Stourbridge. Here Bescot's 42974 is seen cautiously leaving the tunnel with an up working on 27 June 1964. *(Paul Dorney)*

Above: **67.** The 3.20 pm Parcels from Wolverhampton to Stourbridge passes through the ruins of Blowers Green station behind 6967 *Willesley Hall*. This stock would go on to form the 4.55 pm Stourbridge-Worcester local. An insulated six-wheel sausage van features behind the engine, having been picked up at Dudley. 1964. *(John Harris)*

Opposite above: **68.** Another view of the 3.20 pm Parcels as Worcester's 6856 *Stowe Grange* emerges from the 948 yards Dudley Tunnel into the winter sunshine. 1964. *(John Harris)*

Opposite below: **69.** The British Sugar Corporation beet processing factory at Kidderminster gave rise to seasonal traffic in the form of workings of beet from the East of England. 9F 92145, recently transferred from New England to Langwith Junction, is seen on such a working on the frosty morning of 4 January 1965. *(Paul Dorney)*

DUDLEY

70. The northern end of Dudley Tunnel is seen as 7809 *Childrey Manor* emerges with the 4.15 pm Kidderminster-Leamington via Dudley and Great Bridge. The track layout at Dudley precluded down trains passing directly from the OWW on to the South Staffs line and Great Bridge. It was necessary to propel the trains from the down main platform to the up main line via the crossover seen here to gain access to the desired route. *(Peter Reeves)*

71. No such difficulties were experienced by up trains joining the OWW. A Stourbridge 5101 class tank is seen departing from the North Western side of the joint station with the 5.35 pm Birmingham Snow Hill to Brettell Lane. Note the additional brickwork installed around the base of Dudley South Signal Box, probably to provide blast protection against bomb damage during the Second World War. 1962. *(Peter Reeves)*

72. The 5.27 pm Stourbridge-Wolverhampton runs into the down main platform behind 8498 as the 5.29 pm Wolverhampton-Worcester heads for the tunnel behind a 5101 class tank. Railcars and auto trains for Birmingham would normally depart from the bay platform occupied by the box vans. *(Peter Reeves)*

73. A transfer freight from the London Midland Region bound for Stourbridge threads the lines through the station. The train locomotive is Bescot's 48529. As can be seen by the smoke evident over the station buildings heavy trains to Dudley arriving via the South Staffs line also required banking assistance, in this case by LMR bankers from Great Bridge. Dudley North Signal Box can be seen in the far distance above the footbridge. *(Peter Reeves)*

74. The LMR yard (Town Goods) at Dudley is seen being shunted by 7435, during what seems to be extensive relaying works. Behind the train the South Staffs line diverges past Dudley East Signal Box under the Tipton Road Bridge. As a joint station Dudley possessed both upper quadrant signals, operated by the former LNWR East Box, and lower quadrants controlled by the former GWR North and South boxes. *(Thomas Bassindale)*

75. Dudley Station looking south from Tipton Road. The North Western (LMR) station is to the left with the former GWR station to the right. The 1.25 pm Wolverhampton-Hartlebury Parcels is arriving on the up main behind 3778. Over the GW station buildings can be seen the Station Hotel, and opposite, the Hippodrome Theatre, opened in 1938. *(Peter Reeves)*

76. Later that day the Hartlebury Parcels reappears on its return to Wolverhampton, and is seen leaving the down main platform after its five minute booked stop, 5.16-5.21 pm. *(Peter Reeves)*

Above: **77.** No sausage van for collection today as the 3.20 pm Wolverhampton-Stourbridge Parcels leaves the station passing under Birmingham Road bridge behind 45427. Visible through the bridge is Dudley South Signal Box. 1964. *(John Harris)*

Opposite above: **78.** Dudley Zoo was a popular day excursion destination, particularly with the LMR authorities. Excursions from the Western Region were far less common, but a late example is seen here as Tyseley's 6845 *Paviland Grange* gets ready to return the Bank Holiday day trippers to Great Malvern on 3 August 1964, two months after Dudley station had closed to scheduled services. *(Paul Dorney)*

Opposite below: **79.** The last scheduled services from Dudley were the diesel unit trains for Walsall and Lichfield, and the service over the Windmill End Branch to Old Hill. The workings of the latter were shared between single car diesel units and steam-hauled auto trains. The last evening working before closure is seen in the platform at Dudley with Stourbridge's 6434. The last day of services was the following day's 12.26 pm to Old Hill, but unfortunately neither of the two auto-fitted tanks, 6424 and 6434, was available, so the train ran behind 7418, which had to run round the auto trailer at Old Hill for the return. 12 June 1964. *(Paul Dorney)*

Above: **80.** The 6.5 pm Wolverhampton-Stourbridge local is seen at Tipton Five Ways station with 8498. Princes End can be seen in the far distance. The chimney seen on the right belongs to Bean's Foundries, served by the adjacent sidings. At a point just past the far end of these sidings there previously stood Tipton Junction Signal Box, which controlled not only access to Tipton Canal Basin but also a short spur which joined the London & North Western's Stour Valley line. This spur, removed by 1959, was used by the first OWW trains as a means to reach Wolverhampton prior to the opening of what became Wolverhampton Low Level station. c1961. *(Peter Reeves)*

Right: **81.** Between Tipton and Princes End lay sidings serving the South Staffs Wagon Co.'s works, a sister establishment to that at Blowers Green. 3744 shunts the down sidings. *(Peter Reeves)*

Left: **82.** Princes End & Coseley station, which opened slightly later than the others on this section of the line, was a modest affair with wooden platforms and buildings at street level. A down Wolverhampton-bound local stops for custom behind 4173, the locomotive that worked the last scheduled passenger train on the line before closure on 30 July 1962. Dudley's Castle Hill can be seen on the skyline. *(Peter Reeves)*

Below: **83.** The 2.10 pm Wolverhampton-Stourbridge scurries through Princes End behind 7025 *Sudeley Castle* of Shrewsbury shed in around 1961. At this time the 'Castle' would have been diagrammed to work the up 'Cambrian Coast Express' from Shrewsbury to Wolverhampton, and then two locals on the West Midland line. It would return north in the evening with the 5.15 pm Evesham-Crewe Parcels, via the Wombourn Branch. *(Peter Reeves)*

Above: **84.** An afternoon up local, probably the 3.57 pm Wolverhampton-Worcester, is seen leaving Daisy Bank & Bradley station with 4964 *Rodwell Hall* in charge. *(Peter Reeves)*

Opposite above: **85.** Stafford Road's 6418 makes a lively start away from Daisy Bank & Bradley with a Wolverhampton-bound auto-train. Of all the West Midland line stations Daisy Bank always gave the appearance of the most well-tended, with neat flower beds and smart buildings. *(Peter Reeves)*

Opposite below: **86.** Stewart & Lloyd's Bilston Steelworks (Hickman's) at Springvale received daily trains of ironstone from the Oxfordshire and Northamptonshire quarries. Loaded trains were routed via West Bromwich, but the empties usually returned via Dudley and Old Hill. The 5.48 pm Banbury ironstone empties are seen between Bilston and Daisy Bank behind 5361 in around 1958. *(Michael Hale/Great Western Trust)*

87. A down Wolverhampton local slows for the booked stop at Bilston (West) station with 5180 of Stourbridge shed. 11 May 1957. *(Michael Hale/ Great Western Trust)*

88. The West Midland line at Bilston, looking south towards the station. The line veering off to the right leads to the Springvale steelworks. Two panniers assist in the relaying of the down main line, whilst the railcar has probably been employed as transport for the relaying gangs. *(Michael Hale/Great Western Trust)*

89. The 5.27 pm local from Stourbridge to Wolverhampton slows for the Priestfield stop with 8426 in early 1962. Unlike neighbouring lines the West Midland line passenger trains remained exclusively steam-hauled to the end. *(Peter Reeves)*

90. The layout at Priestfield Junction left little doubt as to which line had arrived first. The West Midland line maintains a straight course as it is joined by the line from Birmingham. Old Oak Common's 6021 *King Richard II*, sporting the unique slotted bogie, rounds the sharp curve with the 3.10 pm Paddington-Birkenhead express. c1961. *(Peter Reeves)*

WOLVERHAMPTON

Above: **91.** The six month old 7008 *Swansea Castle* stands in the up main platform at Wolverhampton (Low Level) with the 9.20 am Birkenhead-Bournemouth West comprised of Southern Region coaching stock. A Southern locomotive will replace 7008 at Oxford. The 'Castle' went new to Oxford shed and would remain there for fifteen years. *(David Waldren Collection)*

Opposite above: **92.** Veteran 2927 *Saint Patrick* draws stock from the six-road Carriage Shed which stood alongside the station. Built in 1907, the 'Saint' has a further two years to run before withdrawal from Swindon shed. 9 April 1949. *(David Waldren Collection)*

Opposite below: **93.** 1016 *County of Hants* stands in one of the middle roads with the stock of the 4.55 pm semi-fast train to Chester. Notwithstanding its smart appearance the 'County' was condemned by Shrewsbury shed the following month. September 1963. *(Paul Dorney)*

94. The same train is seen on 3 March 1964 with 6994 *Baggrave Hall*, which has already lost its nameplate, long before the official policy of nameplate removal. Note the change in the Shrewsbury shed code from 89A to 6D, reflecting the transfer of local lines to the London Midland Region. *(Paul Dorney)*

95. The station had only two through platforms, each with a passenger bay platform, and a parcels bay at the southern end of the down platform. Goods lines skirted the station on the eastern side. A down goods, hauled by 5955 *Garth Hall*, is seen in the snows of 1965. The building seen in the far left is the former Midland Railway's Wednesfield Road Goods Depot, to which there was no direct access from Low Level Station. 2 March 1965. *(Paul Dorney)*

96. The 'Inter-City' express, the 4.35 pm Wolverhampton-Paddington, sweeps into the station under Wednesfield Road bridge with 6008 *King James II* in early 1962. The train would have originated in Cannock Road carriage sidings, but already carries headlamps signifying its express passenger status. *(Peter Reeves)*

97. Old Oak Common's 7027 *Thornbury Castle* has charge of the 'Inter-City' as it runs into the up platform in August 1958. A 'Castle' stands in the down bay platform, whilst another waits in the middle road to take over the 2.10 pm Paddington-Birkenhead once the restaurant car has been removed. Meanwhile a Park Royal-bodied trolleybus can be seen crossing the road bridge on its way to Wednesfield. *(David Waldren Collection)*

98. After cessation of West Midland line services in July 1962 the up bay platform was largely given over to parcels traffic, as seen here with Oxley's 3605 in attendance. This part of the station was the one favoured by trainspotters, as a gap in the adjoining buildings allowed also identification of traffic on the LMR High Level lines. 7 March 1964. *(Paul Dorney)*

99. 9658 is seen with a Hawksworth full brake on similar duties in the West Midland bay platform. c1964. *(Author's Collection)*

100. Recently transferred to Stafford Road shed, but still sporting its Old Oak Common shedplate, 9661 proceeds under Wednesfield Road bridge propelling its brake van, probably from Bilston and Stow Heath sidings. The North signal box can be seen through the arches. 1963. *(Paul Dorney)*

101. The last regular steam-hauled service to Paddington ran until the end of the 1964 Summer Timetable, a Fridays-only 5.50 pm from Birmingham Snow Hill. The coaching stock for the service originated in Wolverhampton and 7032 *Denbigh Castle* is seen at the six-road carriage shed behind the station on 12 June 1964. The goods lines referred to earlier can be seen between the shed and the blue brick wall which previously supported the station roof which was removed in the 1930s. *(Paul Dorney)*

Right: **102.** One express from Paddington retained steam haulage until the very end of through services in March 1967. The diesel-hauled 3.10 pm to Shrewsbury undertook an engine change at Low Level for the final stage of its journey. After the mass withdrawal of ex-Great Western tender engines at the end of 1965 the train was usually taken over by a Stanier 5MT provided by Oxley shed, in this case 44659 of Aintree. 12 January 1967. *(Paul Dorney)*

Below: **103.** Stafford Road's sole BR Class 2MT was retained for use with the Divisional Engineer's Saloon, with occasional forays on local passenger services to Stourbridge. It is seen here at the north end of the station preparatory to garaging the saloon in its nearby shed. A 'Castle', 5022 *Wigmore Castle*, can be seen beneath Wednesfield Road bridge waiting to take over a down express. 1962. *(Peter Reeves)*

104. The driver of 1013 *County of Dorset* attends to his charge after its turning on the Stafford Road turntable. It would have arrived on the 2.3 pm Chester-Wolverhampton. *(Simon Dewey)*

105. 6016 *King Edward V* at the Stafford Road coaling plant. The reporting numbers identify it as having worked the 2.10 pm Paddington-Birkenhead as far as Low Level station. The building seen to the right is the Gas Plant, which produced gas that was piped directly to Cannock Road carriage sidings on the far side of the running lines, the gas being used originally for carriage illumination. *(Simon Dewey)*

Opposite above: **106.** Locally-shedded 7014 *Caerhays Castle* stands beneath the coal stage, one of only five 'Castles' to carry the distinctive smokebox-mounted Davies & Metcalfe mechanical lubricator. *(Simon Dewey)*

Opposite below: **107.** The coal stage and turntable were separated from the shed yard and buildings by the Birmingham Canal and the viaduct carrying the LMR's Stour Valley line, prominent here as local resident 7019 *Fowey Castle* comes on shed. The chalked reporting number suggests that it may well have worked the 10.5 am Kingswear-Wolverhampton, with a booked arrival time of 4.38 pm. *(Simon Dewey)*

Above: **108.** Stafford Road shed consisted of two straight-road sheds, relics of an earlier existence as part of the locomotive works of the West Midland Railway, and three roundhouses. In later years two of the roundhouses had fallen into disuse, but the other was retained principally to accommodate tank engines. Seen emerging from the No.1 surviving roundhouse is Bristol Bath Road's 3677, evidently recently outshopped from 'the Factory'. Ex-works locomotives were frequently tested on local services before being returned to their home sheds. c1959. *(Author's Collection)*

109. One cannot help but admire the operating and maintenance staff who were required to turn out locomotives for premier express services in such primitive working conditions as prevailed at Stafford Road. 5063 *Earl Baldwin* is in the old No.4 shed known as 'the Arcade' whilst another 'Castle' can be glimpsed in the adjoining No.5 shed, the old broad gauge locomotive shed. It is telling that when diesel-hydraulics arrived to work the expresses in place of steam they were sent to the more modern and spacious Oxley. *(Author's Collection)*

110. Looking smartly turned out and ready for the road in the Lower Yard at its home shed is 6011 *King James I.* 1960. *(Author's Collection)*

111. The majority of Stafford Road's 'Kings' were put in store at the end of the 1962 Summer Timetable, coaled and ready for further use if required. The call never came and 6017 *King Edward IV* and its shedmates made a short last trip in the New Year to the breakers, Cox & Danks at Langley Green. *(Author's Collection)*

112. The 'Kings' were for many years banned from proceeding beyond Wolverhampton, but bridge works enabled the restriction to be rescinded in April 1959. Thereafter they were permitted to work to Shrewsbury, and a 'King' was regularly rostered to work the premier train to there, the 'Cambrian Coast Express', the 10.10 am Paddington-Aberystwyth and Pwllheli. Here 6024 *King Edward I* is seen at Dunstall Park station with the down train shortly after authority was granted. The train appears to be making an unscheduled stop as the guard in the leading brake has his door partly opened. Stafford Road shed lies immediately over the wall to the right of the picture. *(Author's Collection)*

113. Between Dunstall Park station and Oxley Viaduct lay Stafford Road Junction where the line in the foreground diverged to Victoria Basin Goods yard and the Locomotive Works. Longstanding local resident 7026 *Tenby Castle* is seen working a short up express past the junction signal box. *(Michael Hale/Great Western Trust)*

Stafford Road Locomotive Works' origins lay in the Shrewsbury & Birmingham (S&B) Railway which established its headquarters and workshops in the town. The Great Western Railway's amalgamation with the S&B in 1854 and subsequently the West Midland Railway in 1863 resulted in an expansion of the facilities, and locomotive building commenced under the direction of Joseph Armstrong, who in addition had to deal with the GWR's acquired narrow gauge stock. The works was always handicapped by its awkward site, with shops on both sides of the Stafford Road, and in time the decision was made to cease the manufacture of new locomotives at Wolverhampton and undertake all new construction at Swindon. The last locomotive rolled out in 1908. Nonetheless Stafford Road continued to be an important repair facility, second only to Swindon in importance, and in the 1930s it was expanded and modernised. All types of repair were undertaken to locomotives from throughout the Western Region, although 'heavy' repairs to 'Kings', even those allocated locally, required a trip to Swindon. Lack of space prevented the modernised works being laid out on the Swindon and Caerphilly models with transverse repair bays and traverser. There were instead three longitudinal bays, with two devoted to repairs and the third used as the machine shop. Inevitably, in consequence of the change to diesel power and the reduction in need for steam repair capacity during the 1950s, the works was found to be surplus to requirements and closed in 1964.

114. A general view of the 1930s Erecting Shop, with identifiable locomotives 2294, 8424, and 5658. *(Michael Hale/Great Western Trust)*

115. Neath's 7739 was withdrawn in November 1962, but became one of a number sold to London Transport (LT) for engineering train use. It is seen at the Works in 1963 prior to overhaul and subsequent delivery to LT, where as L98 it gave six years' further service until scrapped in 1969. *(Simon Dewey)*

116. Few locomotives were cut up at the Works. One exception was 5938 *Stanley Hall*, which arrived for repair in early 1963 and was promptly condemned. The cylinder damage which occasioned its demise can be seen in the photograph as it stands outside the 1930s repair shop. It served as a stationary boiler throughout that summer and was then quietly despatched. *(Simon Dewey)*

117. 3802 went through the shops in 1963 and is seen by the weighhouse after its repair, from which it appears by the chalk marks to carry the boiler cladding, and possibly the boiler, from 2855, a 28XX which had been cut up at the works in the previous February. October 1963. *(Author's Collection)*

118. Oxley shed lay to the west of extensive yards at the northern edge of the town. It was a Churchward double roundhouse, with sufficient land for the erection of a third, which was never required. It was principally allocated goods and mixed traffic locomotives although it acquired some 'Castles' on the closure of Stafford Road in September 1963. Oxley's own 6831 *Bearley Grange* is seen in the yard with another of the class. *(Author's Collection)*

119. One of Oxley's small stud of pannier tanks stands beneath the coal stage. 9768 spent its entire thirty year existence at this one shed. *(Author's Collection)*

120. As goods and mixed traffic types predominated at Oxley the shed was not renowned for the cleanliness of its locomotives. 7806 *Cockington Manor* provides a stark example in this 1964 photograph. The 'gallows' construction which can be seen at the roundhouse entrance was part of a regime to warn footplate men of the dangers of the newly-erected 25kv overhead wires as Oxley crews would regularly work goods trains to Crewe. *(Author's Collection)*

121. The land acquired for possible expansion is evident in this view of 2895 at the rear of the roundhouse. As the standard class of Great Western heavy goods locomotive, a number of these locomotives was always to be found allocated to the shed. *(John Harris)*

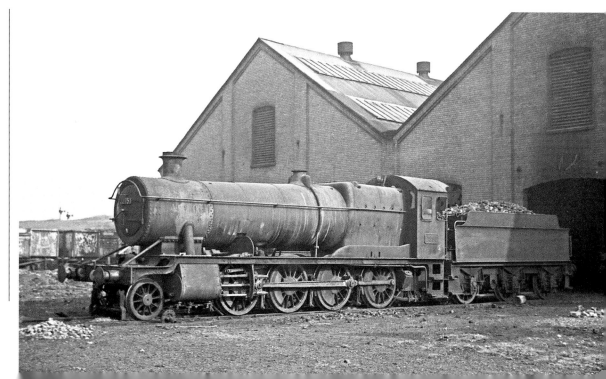

122. After the transfer of the local Western Region lines to the LMR in 1963 other classes became more commonplace. Tyseley's 92118 stands alongside the shed on 29 October 1966. *(Paul Dorney)*

123. Withdrawn the previous month, the work of 6823 *Oakley Grange* is over. It is prepared for removal by 7924 *Thornycroft Hall* on the first stage of its journey to be cut up at Bird's scrapyard, Long Marston. 9 August 1965. *(Paul Dorney)*

Opposite above: 124. The last years of steam saw many locomotives temporarily visit Oxley en route to the local scrapyards, particularly to Cashmore's at Great Bridge. 47272 from Birkenhead gives an appearance of being in steam, but the absence of coupling rods gives the game away. It was scrapped at Bird's, Long Marston. 29 October 1966. *(Paul Dorney)*

Opposite below: 125. The Wombourne Branch left the main line at a triangular junction at the northern extremity of Oxley sidings. It can be seen here diverging left as 6934 *Beachamwell Hall* approaches the yard with an up 'C' class fitted goods. Oxley North Signal Box can just be discerned above the two buffer stops. *(Michael Hale/Great Western Trust)*

Above: 126. One line of the triangular junction was carried on a short three arch viaduct crossing the Staffordshire & Worcestershire Canal, seen here as Stourbridge's 4326 takes the down main with what is probably the Saturdays-only 10.0 am Round Oak-Crewe 'F' class unfitted goods. *(Author's Collection)*

THE WOMBOURN BRANCH

127. 6925 *Hackness Hall* is seen awaiting the road at Oxley Branch Junction with the 11.0 am Crewe-Bristol West class 'C' goods. The large factory in the background is Courtauld's, which boasted its own internal railway system connected to the branch.
(Simon Dewey)

The branch had its origins in the initial Parliamentary Bill for the Oxford, Worcester and Wolverhampton Railway, which proposed the construction of a branch line from Brettell Lane to Kingswinford. The branch opened in 1858 and by 1860 had been extended to the Earl of Dudley's coalfields near Lower Gornal. In the early twentieth century the Great Western Railway proposed building a branch from Oxley to Bridgnorth, but commercial considerations and the outbreak of war caused a revision of its plans. The line to Baggeridge, which served local mines, would be extended to Oxley, where it would join the Wolverhampton-Shrewsbury line at a triangular junction. The branch opened as a through route in 1925, with single track from Oxley Branch Junction to Baggeridge Junction and double track thereafter to Kingswinford Junction, with brick built stations at Tettenhall, Wombourn and Himley, and Halts with pagoda waiting facilities at Compton, Penn, Gornal, Pensnett, Bromley and Brockmoor. There was one passing loop at Wombourn. Passenger services were poorly patronised and lasted only until 1932, but the line proved useful keeping through traffic away from the congested routes through the Black Country.

128. The same working is seen getting away from a signal check at the junction behind 6982 *Melmerby Hall* as a Corporation bus makes its way along Aldersley Road. *(Simon Dewey)*

129. An unidentified up 'H' class goods is seen at Wombourn station with 6946 *Heatherden Hall* . Through trains would often take water here, being unlikely to delay any other traffic. 8 February 1964. *(David Wilson)*

130. A coming storm threatens further rain as 44941 passes Wombourn's down fixed distant signal with the 10.35 pm Tavistock Junction-Crewe goods shortly before the line's closure. Sheeted wagons of china clay destined for the Potteries were a regular feature of this train. 9 January 1965. *(Paul Dorney)*

131. After closure of the line as a through route the section to Baggeridge Junction was retained to serve Baggeridge Colliery. An afternoon coal working is seen awaiting departure behind 8718. The decrepit Baggeridge Junction Signal Box, where the single line to Oxley commenced, can be seen in the distance. 3 June 1966. *(Paul Dorney)*

132. Two Hunslet 'Austerity' saddle tanks, Nos.8 and 9 (3776/7 of 1952), went new to Baggeridge Colliery and worked the colliery branch from the junction until its closure. The engine led its train down the incline from the colliery whilst the return was always propelled. No.8 is here seen in the exchange sidings. After closure of the pit in 1969 the two tank engines left under their own steam to take up new duties in the Cannock coalfield. Both were subsequently preserved. 1 July 1966. *(Paul Dorney)*

133. The exchange siding with the colliery lay a short distance off the main line. 9608 struggles up the short connection with a string of loaded wagons. 23 June 1966. *(Paul Dorney)*

134. The 11.0 am Crewe-Bristol 'C' class goods is seen once more in the weeks before closure with 6854 *Roundhill Grange* of Oxley shed between Baggeridge Junction and Gornal Halt. 23 January 1965. (Paul Dorney)

135. In addition to the colliery traffic Stourbridge Bank Train No.18 served the trading estate at Pensnett. Considerable traffic was generated by the local brick and tile works, including the frequent appearance of Italian State Railway (FS) box vans which had come to the UK by train ferry. Examples are seen here with 4646 on 29 June 1965. *(Paul Dorney)*

136. 8718 makes lively progress past the much overgrown island platform of the long-closed Pensnett Halt with a train of coal empties on 2 July 1966. The bridge in the background carries the main Dudley-Kingswinford road. *(Paul Dorney)*

137. A domestic coal concentration depot was established in May 1964 at the Pensnett Trading Estate by the firm Lunt, Comley and Pitt. Stourbridge's 6683 is seen awaiting permission to proceed to the estate to discharge its load. Behind the train lies the private siding of Gibbon's Lenches Bridge works, where the Talyllyn Railway's No.1 underwent a comprehensive rebuilding in 1958. *(Paul Dorney)*

138. The platforms at Bromley Halt, closed in 1932, are still evident as 3607 makes its way back from Pensnett en route to Stourbridge Yard on 29 June 1966. The line to Baggeridge Junction was singled the following year. *(Paul Dorney)*

139. The basin of the Stourbridge Extension Canal features prominently as 73038 of Chester shed heads north through Bromley with the 2.30 pm Rowley Regis-Saltney train of oil empties. The Cookley Works of Richard Thomas and Baldwin dominate the skyline, and a healthy string of wagons occupies the sidings at the Bromley Basin canal wharf. 13 October 1956. *(Michael Hale/Great Western Trust)*

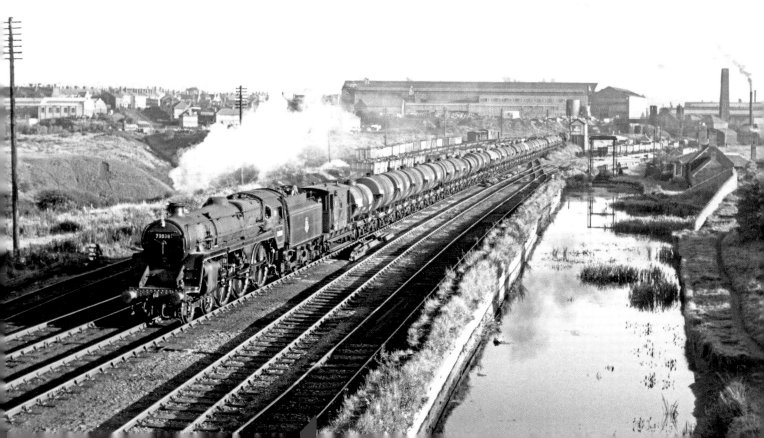

140. Bank Train No.18 is seen between Bromley and Brockmoor behind 3607. The chimneys are those of yet more brickworks and of the Cookley Works. 29 June 1966. *(Paul Dorney)*

141. Doubleheaded pannier tanks 4696 and 4646 do the honours at Brockmoor with a long train of coal empties from the Pensnett coal concentration yard as they approach Kingswinford Junction, the yard of which can be seen to the right. 14 May 1966. *(Paul Dorney)*

142. 3607 leaves the Wombourn Branch and rejoins the erstwhile Oxford, Worcester and Wolverhampton metals at Kingswinford Junction South. 7 May 1966. *(Paul Dorney)*

PRIESTFIELD-BIRMINGHAM

The Birmingham, Wolverhampton & Dudley Railway was a scheme put forward by the promoters of the Birmingham & Oxford Junction Railway who saw the advantages to be gained by extending their line through to Wolverhampton. In 1848 a Parliamentary Act authorised the amalgamation of the two companies, and their acquisition by the Great Western Railway in accordance with an earlier agreement. Construction was delayed by the inevitable objections of the London and North Western Railway, but the B&O opened as a mixed gauge line in October 1852. The section to Priestfield where it joined the West Midland line opened in November 1854 and thereafter the GWR favoured this route through Birmingham as providing the best opportunity to achieve its goal of running through trains from Paddington to the Mersey.

143. Returning to the junction at Priestfield we see 6019 *King Henry V* rounding the curve with a Birkenhead-Paddington express, on its way from Shrewsbury. It still carries the reporting number from having worked the down 'Cambrian Coast Express'. 1962. *(Peter Reeves)*

144. Stourbridge's 9613 makes heavy weather of an up pick-up goods as it struggles through Priestfield during the winter of 1961. *(Peter Reeves)*

145. A Summer Saturday extra passes Bilston Central station behind an unidentified 'Modified Hall'. The majority of the stations on this section followed the same pattern, with an impressive Italianate building with booking office and waiting facilities on the up side and a modest waiting shelter on the down. *(Michael Hale/Great Western Trust)*

146. A lightweight down goods train heads for Wolverhampton. The painted wheels and smokebox suggest that 6667 has recently paid a visit to the works and may well be on a proving run. Sankey's Bankfield Works can be seen to the right of the signal box. *(Author's Collection)*

147. Chance & Hunt's chemical works and the steelworks of the Patent Shaft & Axletree Company dominate the background as a 'Hall' with an up goods gets the signal for the loop, crossing the Walsall Canal and approaching Wednesbury North Signal Box. A pannier tank attends to the down sidings. *(Michael Hale/Great Western Trust)*

148. The pannier tanks acquired by London Transport (LT) would visit BR workshops when overhaul was required. L93 (previously 7779, sold to LT in 1958) has received works attention at Stafford Road and has been enlisted to work a local bank train by way of test. It is seen alongside the Patent Shaft Brunswick Works. *(Author's Collection)*

149. The majestic 47XX mixed traffic 2-8-0s were regulars on the line with the fast fitted goods between London and Birkenhead, but customarily passed through at times inconvenient for photographers. Here 4708 has been captured as it heads north through Wednesbury with what is probably the 6.48 am Old Oak Common-Oxley Sidings 'D' class partly fitted goods. The rear of the train is crossing the bridge under which passes the South Staffs Dudley-Walsall line. *(David Wilson)*

150. A young trainspotter jumps for joy as 6808 *Beenham Grange*, previously of Penzance shed, works an up fully-fitted goods through Wednesbury, and begins the climb to the tunnel at Swan Village. The chimneys of the Patent Shaft Works, known locally to some as 'the Seven Sisters', can be seen in the background. April 1964. *(Paul Dorney)*

151. Longstanding Stafford Road resident 6006 *King George I* is seen on the final approach to the Tunnel with the 3.35 pm Wolverhampton-Paddington express on 10 April 1960. *King George I* was the first of the 'Kings' to be withdrawn, in February 1962. It was cut up at Swindon Works almost immediately. *(Terry Hyde)*

152. The view from Hill Top looking towards West Bromwich was dominated by the massive Swan Village Gas Works. A long train of empty coaching stock drifts down towards the tunnel behind Tyseley's 6971 *Athelhampton Hall* on 2 June 1962. *(Terry Hyde)*

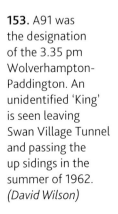

153. A91 was the designation of the 3.35 pm Wolverhampton-Paddington. An unidentified 'King' is seen leaving Swan Village Tunnel and passing the up sidings in the summer of 1962. *(David Wilson)*

154. The signalman at Swan Village North Signal Box has timed to perfection when to return the signals to danger in order to allow the reopening of the gates at this busy level crossing at Swan Lane. The train is the 10.50 am Wolverhampton-Margate on 13 June 1964. Later in the journey 7012 *Barry Castle* will be replaced by a Southern Region locomotive and will make its way back to Wolverhampton with the return set. *(Paul Dorney)*

155. An up Class 'C' fully-fitted goods hurries through the snow at Swan Village with 6989 *Wightwick Hall* of Gloucester shed, on 2 February 1963. *(David Wilson)*

Above: 156. Engineering work on the down main line has brought 3203 to Guns Village, between Swan Village and West Bromwich. The signals are the home signals of Swan Village South box with the Great Bridge branch home signal, and the lower one for the Gasworks Yard. *(Peter Reeves)*

Opposite above: 157. The branch platforms are seen in this view of Swan Village looking towards Great Bridge. Shunting is taking place in the Gasworks yard with 3756. The modern signal box is Swan Village West, which controlled another level crossing over Swan Lane. On the skyline the cooling towers of Ocker Hill Power Station can be seen. *(Michael Hale/Great Western Trust)*

Opposite below: 158. The Great Bridge branch provided a connection between Swan Village and the South Staffs line from Walsall to Dudley. The Great Western had running powers over the section to Dudley and the Western Region continued with the arrangement after nationalisation for Dudley-Birmingham services. Railcar W8 is seen at Great Bridge (South) with a Birmingham-bound working. The works in the background are those of Horseley Bridge & Thomas Piggott, responsible for construction of many canal and railway bridges. The works closed in 1992. *(Michael Hale/Great Western Trust)*

159. Passing the large London & North Western Railway Grain Shed on the final approach to Dudley on South Staffs metals is 4146 with the 5.35 pm Birmingham-Brettell Lane. This was one of three possible routes for travel from Birmingham to Dudley by train, the alternatives being via Old Hill and Windmill End, or using the LMR route from Birmingham New Street via Dudley Port. *(Michael Hale/ Great Western Trust)*

160. The 11.40 am Birkenhead-Paddington threads the cutting at Guns Village and approaches West Bromwich behind 6019 *King Henry V* in the summer of 1962. The signals visible in the distance are those of Swan Village South Signal Box, junction for the Great Bridge line. *(Peter Reeves)*

161. The 9.20 am Birkenhead-Bournemouth, comprised of Southern coaching stock, passes under Lyng Lane bridge and enters West Bromwich station in the hands of Oxford's 7008 *Swansea Castle,* which since the 1948 view of the same train at Wolverhampton has acquired a double chimney. c1962. *(Peter Reeves)*

162. A Banbury-Bilston iron ore train struggles through West Bromwich behind 6324 in May 1957. The train will run into Stow Heath sidings and then be taken down the West Midland line to the steel works at Springvale. *(Michael Hale/ Great Western Trust)*

163. The signalman at West Bromwich Signal Box takes advantage of a lull in main line traffic to allow shunting to get under way as 75000, displaying its newly applied green livery, prepares to make a delivery of coal to the down side goods yard. *(Peter Reeves)*

164. Leamington shed's 8109, another of the 1938 rebuilds, departs from the station with a short up parcels. *(Peter Reeves)*

165. A91, the 3.35 pm Wolverhampton-Paddington, must have departed punctually from Low Level station as it is recorded by the clock on West Bromwich's Trinity Church as right on time, with 6021 *King Richard II*. *(Peter Reeves)*

166. A short section of the down main line is being relayed between West Bromwich and Handsworth Junction as 5375 heads an up coal train past the unconcerned gangers. The flat area to the left was the site of sidings of the closed Sandwell Colliery. *(Eric Rogers)*

167. From Handsworth Junction, where the line from Stourbridge joined, it became a four-track railway to Birmingham. The 11.10 am Paddington-Birkenhead is going well as it passes Handsworth & Smethwick station on the fast lines behind 7026 *Tenby Castle* in March 1959. *(Michael Hale/Great Western Trust)*

168. A down local pick-up goods, probably bound for the yard at Oldbury & Langley Green, is seen on the relief lines at Handsworth & Smethwick with Tyseley shed's 3625 in around 1964. *(Author's Collection)*

169. A down 'K' class goods travelling on the down main behind 4167, possibly the 10.26 am Bordesley Junction-Dudley, is seen from Queen's Head Signal Box. The bridge visible towards the rear of the train carries the LMR's Soho-Perry Barr line, linking the Stour Valley and Grand Junction routes. *(Author's Collection)*

170. A Dudley-Birmingham auto passes Soho & Winson Green Signal Box as it leaves behind 1458. At this time the services were shared between auto-trains and railcars. 1957. *(Author's Collection)*

171. Tyseley's 7908 *Henshall Hall* sweeps hurriedly under Norton Street bridge, between Hockley and Soho & Winson Green stations, with a down express. *(Author's Collection)*

172. The 7.35 am Birkenhead-Margate enters Hockley behind Chester's 5061 *Earl of Birkenhead* in around 1956. Locomotives from Chester and Oxford sheds alternated daily on this service. Hockley had extensive goods facilities on both sides of the four through lines, but the station had only three platform faces. The impressive baroque-style building on the skyline is surprisingly that of a local bakery, Scribban's. *(Keith Tilbrook)*

173. The 'King Commemorative Tour' of 17 November 1962 provided one of the last outings for these fine locomotives. 6018 *King Henry VI* is seen at Hockley presenting the passengers with an opportunity for photographs. The tour proceeded to Wolverhampton behind the 'King', there then followed a trip across the Wombourn Branch to Stourbridge with 6631. The return to London involved a journey down the Great Western/Great Central Joint line with 2210. *(Author's Collection)*

174. A Saturday extra from the South Coast is seen from Hockley South Signal Box, emerging from the tunnels after leaving Snow Hill behind 5987 *Brocket Hall*. 1963. *(John Harris)*

***Above*: 175.** Birmingham Snow Hill station looking north. A Paddington express of Great Western stock climbs majestically from the Hockley tunnels behind 7026 *Tenby Castle*. To the left can be seen Birmingham North Signal Box, a 1910 installation involving Siemen's power interlocking. Similar equipment was in use at Birmingham South and Hockley North boxes. 1953. *(Author's Collection)*

***Opposite above*: 176.** Running into Platform 7 in around 1952 we see Stafford Road's 6005 *King George II* with an up Paddington express. The 'King' sports the short-lived blue livery which was allocated by British Railways to express passenger locomotives at the time. It was found to be unsuitable due to excessive weathering, so consequently Brunswick Green, a dark green akin to the former Great Western livery, was adopted instead. *(Thomas Bassindale)*

***Opposite below*: 177.** Landore's 5958 *Knolton Hall* waits impatiently for departure with the 3.45 pm Snow Hill-Swansea in around 1955. It will travel down the North Warwick line to Cheltenham and follow the Severn estuary to South Wales, unlike most Birmingham-Cardiff trains which went via Worcester and Hereford. A sister 'Hall' can be seen in Platform 12 with the 4.0 pm to Paddington via Oxford. *(Keith Tilbrook)*

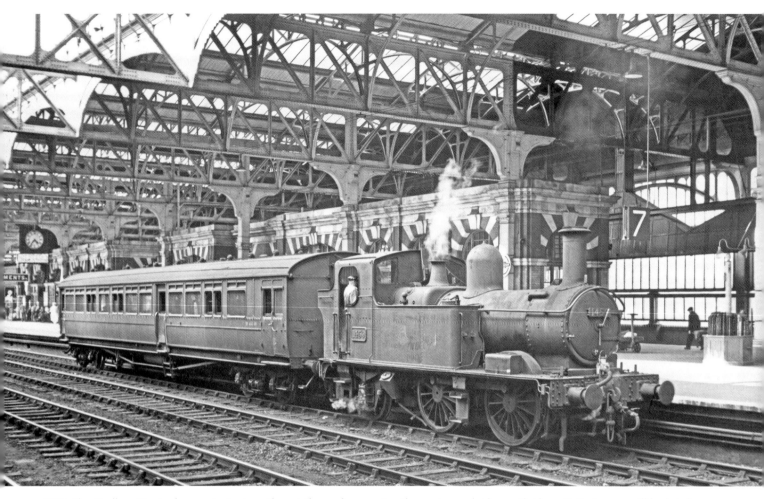

178. The Dudley-Birmingham auto is given the privilege of occupying the main up platform, Platform 7. Its tenure will be brief, departing again at 4.55 pm to make way for the up 'Inter City' due shortly afterwards. 1459 has charge of aged trailer car W44, of 1906. 1 June 1957. *(Michael Hale/Great Western Trust)*

179. A Snow Hill-Wolverhampton local is seen in Platform 1 with 3104, another of the pre-war rebuilds of earlier Churchward locomotives with larger boiler and smaller wheels. 1955. *(Henry Casserley)*

180. In May 1955 the Western Region authorities borrowed a Stanier Pacific from Camden shed to assess the desirability and benefits of equipping the 'Kings' with double blastpipes and chimneys. 46237 *City of Bristol* worked the 9.10 am Paddington-Wolverhampton and 12.35 pm return. It is seen here in Platform 7 on the return working with the old Great Western dynamometer car W7 of 1901. Note the additional spoked wheel for speed recording alongside the wheeltapper. *(Keith Tilbrook)*

181. A Paddington-Birkenhead express stands in Platform 6 at Snow Hill behind 6014 *King Henry VII* in around 1959. The 'King' is the example which was subjected to a half-hearted attempt at the then fashionable streamlining craze in the 1930s. In consequence of its 'bull nose' it was adapted to accommodate the reporting number frame below the smokebox, a feature it retained with its altered cab until withdrawal in 1962. *(Thomas Bassindale)*

182. The summer of 1964 saw the last widespread use of the 'Castle' class locomotives. A down Saturday extra is seen in Platform 5 with 4082 *Windsor Castle* in charge. At the time the station was suffering some upheaval from the work connected with the widening of Great Charles Street. 8 August 1964. *(Paul Burchill)*

183. The two through tracks enabled goods trains to avoid the platform lines and to be held to allow expresses to pass. What appears to be a weedkilling train, comprising an adapted Churchward 'Toplight' in use as accommodation, a tank wagon and former ROD Great Central tenders, is held on the down through at the north end of the station behind 4111 of Tyseley shed. c1960. *(Author's Collection)*

SMETHWICK TO STOURBRIDGE AND BRANCHES

In 1860 construction was authorised by Parliament of a line from Stourbridge to Old Hill. An extension to these powers was granted the following year to the Stourbridge Railway (Extension) Company taking the line from Old Hill to join the London & North Western Railway at Smethwick. The line to Cradley Heath, including the goods branches to Corngreaves and Hayes Lane, opened in 1863 with Old Hill following in 1866. The section from Old Hill to the LNWR at Smethwick was completed to the satisfaction of the Board of Trade by April 1867, allowing through running to Birmingham New Street station. Meanwhile, powers obtained by the Great Western Railway had enabled a line to be constructed to a junction on the Birmingham, Wolverhampton & Dudley at Handsworth, to permit trains to run to Snow Hill station. This too opened on 1 April 1867.

184. At Smethwick West up trains from Stourbridge normally proceeded to Handsworth Junction and Snow Hill, but as mentioned above a connection existed to the LMR's Stour Valley line at Galton Junction. Stourbridge's 5167 is seen taking the Galton Junction line in around 1957 with what is probably a football special bound for Witton and the Aston Villa ground. This connection was severed in 1961 and remained so until 1966 when it was reinstated to allow Stourbridge line services to run into Birmingham New Street station and thus facilitate the closure of Snow Hill. *(Eric Rogers)*

Above: **185.** The 5.40 pm all stations from Snow Hill to Stourbridge draws to a halt at Smethwick West station behind 7027 *Thornbury Castle* of Worcester shed. A diverse complement of workers in contrasting fashions awaits this rush hour service. 1962. *(Peter Reeves)*

Opposite above: **186.** Unlike at Smethwick, the next station at Oldbury & Langley Green boasted a yard of sidings serving Messrs Cox & Danks, where the 'Kings' from Stafford Road were cut up, and the works of British Industrial Plastics, and the short branch to Oldbury Town seen in the foreground. By the time of this photograph the branch had been cut back to Albright & Wilson's chemical works. 45275 is seen setting back into the yard with a train which includes wagons of phosphate rock for Albright's. 1965. *(Author's Collection)*

Opposite below: **187.** Until replaced by diesel multiple units in 1958 the 5101 tanks were the customary power for local passenger trains. 4154 is seen at Oldbury & Langley Green station with a down local for Stourbridge. The booking office is at street level, adjacent to a bridge over the Oldbury Town Branch. 25 May 1957. *(Michael Hale/Great Western Trust)*

Above: 188. The Midland branch of the Stephenson Locomotive Society, under the direction of the celebrated W.A. Camwell, was well known for organising enthusiasts' specials, particularly farewell trips for threatened lines and locomotive classes. One such, a last trip to Swindon behind the final surviving 'County', 1011 *County of Chester*, is seen at Rowley Regis & Blackheath on Sunday, 20 September 1964. *(Author's Collection)*

Opposite above: 189. A down Stourbridge local slows for the Rowley Regis stop with 4170. The booking facilities here were in a building on the adjoining road bridge, the platforms having only modest waiting shelters. An oil terminal was situated at Rowley Regis and regular workings brought supplies both from Thameshaven and Ellesmere Port. 20 May 1957. *(Michael Hale/Great Western Trust)*

Opposite below: 190. The summit of the climb from Stourbridge can be seen here within the tunnel at Old Hill. Rowley Regis station lies at the far end. 4696 has arrived at the head of a goods from Stourbridge Yard, banked by a similar locomotive which will now lead the train down the Halesowen Branch. 1966. *(David Waldren Collection)*

THE HALESOWEN BRANCH

The branch to Halesowen was constructed under powers obtained by the Great Western Railway in 1872, which had by that time taken over the Stourbridge Railway. Originally envisaged as a through railway from Dudley to Halesowen, the line was built as two separate branches, and the junction layout at Old Hill precluded any through running of services. Both sections opened in 1878. A short branch to the canal basin, from a junction just short of Halesowen station, opened in 1902. The significance of Halesowen as an industrial centre was confirmed by a further scheme,

in the name of the Halesowen Railway, to link Halesowen with the Midland Railway's Birmingham to Gloucester line. The agreement provided that the line would be worked jointly by the MR and GWR companies, using the latter company's station at Halesowen. This line opened in 1883, with intermediate stations at Rubery and Hunnington. In 1905 the Austin Motor Works was established at the site of the junction with the Midland Railway. Thereafter this generated most of the traffic on the joint line, which during the 1950s included van trains of steel body panels from the Pressed Steel works at Swindon, and special workmen's services. The joint section from Halesowen station to the motor works closed completely in 1964.

Opposite: 191. Through workmen's services to the Austin Motor Company works at Longbridge ceased in August 1958. Because of weight restrictions over Dowery Dell Viaduct they were latterly monopolised by 74XX panniers, a number of which were maintained by Stourbridge shed specifically for the purpose. On 20 August 1957 7449 is seen after arrival at Halesowen station with the 5.9 pm from Longbridge. *(Michael Hale/Great Western Trust)*

Above: 192. After closure of the joint line to Longbridge the Branch was maintained to serve Halesowen and the Hawne Canal Basin, with traffic from the Coombs Wood Tube Works of Stewarts and Lloyds. Steel tubes were carried from the works by canal to the transhipment shed to be carried forward by train. In this 1966 photograph 4696 is seen at the Basin with such traffic. *(David Waldren Collection)*

THE WINDMILL END BRANCH

193. The 12.26 pm Saturdays-only from Dudley arrives behind 7414, not fitted for auto-working, which consequently will be required to run round the trailer before the return. 1964. *(Author's Collection)*

The Windmill End Branch, known locally as 'the Bumble Hole', left Old Hill at the Stourbridge end of the up platform. It was opened on 1 March 1878 by the Great Western Railway and was double track throughout with, at the time of opening, one station at Windmill End. This was complemented in 1905 with the opening of halts at Baptist End, Darby End and Old Hill (High Street). The station at Windmill End was reduced to 'halt' status in 1952. Steeply graded throughout, there was an intermediate signal box at Cox's Lane. Another opened in 1879 at Windmill End Junction, when the line to Withymoor Basin was commissioned. The line was useful as a diversionary route when the B,W&D was obstructed, having the same availability as the OWW main line, ie a red route, open to all GWR locomotives other than the 'Kings' and the 47XXs.

194. The branch was well known for its undulating formation, with steep gradients in both directions and a noticeable 'dip' shown to good effect in this view of the unlikely combination of Birkenhead's 92113 piloting 35026 *Lamport & Holt Line* between Cox's Lane Crossing and Old Hill (High Street). The train was the Warwickshire Railway Society's three day 'Aberdonian' railtour, which had evidently taken a somewhat unorthodox route back from the Granite City. 26 June 1966. *(Paul Dorney)*

195. At Windmill End Junction a short branch left for Withymoor Canal Basin, known also as Netherton Goods. Oxley Bank Train 31, the 1.15 pm Saturdays-only, is seen leaving the branch behind 3782 on 29 May 1965. During this period the branch saw traffic only during the day, with the junction signal box being switched out overnight. *(Paul Dorney)*

***Above*: 196.** The branch served a yard and a large transhipment shed which covered the canal basin, and the traffic latterly comprised mainly pig iron and boiler plate for the chain-making and boilermaking local firms such as Noah Hingley's and H.& T. Danks. In this late view, just before closure on 5 July 1965, Stourbridge's 9614 appears to have little to do before returning to its duties at Blowers Green Yard. 9 June 1965. *(Paul Dorney)*

***Opposite above*: 197.** Immediately before the yard there was a gated crossing of Northfield Road. The young fireman of 3744 is allowed to handle the shunting manoeuvres as it marshals its train for the return to Oxley Sidings. As can be seen, traffic was sufficiently heavy in earlier days to warrant the provision of a footbridge. 11 June 1965. *(Paul Dorney)*

***Opposite below*: 198.** 9614 is now seen having crossed Northfield Road to take water before returning to Blowers Green. What may well be Netherton's only classical graffiti artist appears to have been at work on the footbridge. 9 June 1965. *(Paul Dorney)*

199. The 10.26 am Bordesley Junction-Round Oak storms past Windmill End Junction behind a dishevelled looking 6633. In early 1965 the former Great Western locomotives suffered the indignity of the removal of their name and numberplates. Nevertheless, the authorities at Tyseley shed seem determined that despite that no one should doubt that the number is 6633 and that it is one of theirs. 12 April 1965. *(Paul Dorney)*

200. The 12.45 pm Saturdays-only Old Hill-Dudley auto gets away from its last intermediate stop at Baptist End Halt with 6424, three weeks before the withdrawal of the service. 23 May 1964. *(Paul Dorney)*

201. 3631 with the No.31 Bank Train, the 2.7 pm Netherton-Oxley Sidings, waits impatiently at Windmill End Junction's starter as 92046 heads for Rowley Regis with an up oil train. 1965. *(John Harris)*

202. Another 9F, 92111 of Birkenhead shed, is seen shortly after passing Blowers Green Junction with the 4.35 am Ellesmere Port-Rowley Regis oil. It will stop at the branch starting signal and await the arrival of a banker. 1964. *(John Harris)*

203. The crew of 48762 is advised by Blowers Green Junction that a banker is on its way, to assist with the trip over the branch with a Warrington-Langley Green train of imported phosphate rock, used by Albright & Wilson's in phosphorus production at their Oldbury Works. 22 May 1965. *(Paul Dorney)*

204. Stourbridge's 6656 has now arrived to assist, and will bank the train through to Rowley Regis, coupled to the brake van as the trip involves both falling and rising gradients. Down trains would normally receive their banker at Cox's Lane Crossing, 'in the dip', and would then bank uncoupled through to Blowers Green. *(Paul Dorney)*

205. The daily 10.26 am Bordesley-Round Oak on the last part of the branch, approaching Blowers Green Junction behind 4175, banked by a 56XX. The large premises behind are those of the South Staffs Wagon Repair Company. 11 August 1965. *(Paul Dorney)*

206. The aforementioned train from Bordesley Yard could produce all manner of locomotives. Here 92002 of Tyseley shed is seen at Blowers Green Junction, preparing to place a detached wagon in the yard for repair at the wagon works. 10 June 1965. *(Paul Dorney)*

207. With the shunting now complete 92002 has rejoined its train and prepares to depart for Dudley. The banana vans were regular traffic on this service, destined for the banana ripening sheds at Dudley Castle (WR) Goods Yard. *(Paul Dorney)*

208. Returning to Old Hill we see an auto train from Dudley in the up platform at the station on 6 April 1957. At this time the working was a diagram of Stafford Road shed, but for the last two years of the service the duty was transferred to Stourbridge, and the locomotives transferred there too. It is to be hoped that no prospective passenger for Halesowen is misled by the station board, as public services to there ceased in 1927. *(Michael Hale/Great Western Trust)*

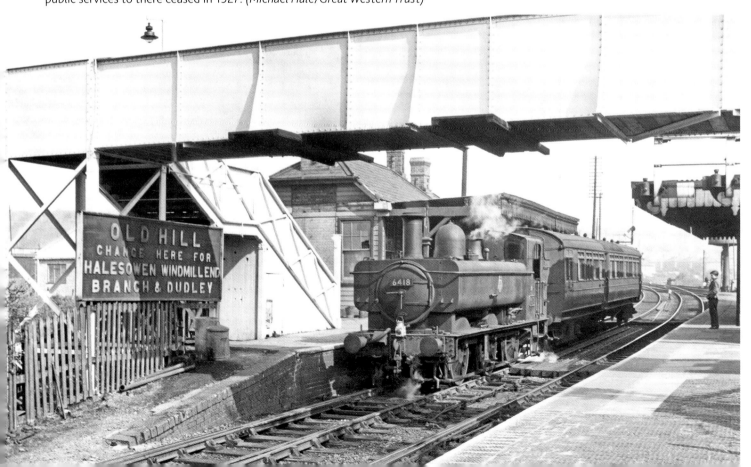

209. A later view of the same train in 1964 reveals how the Halesowen branch at the north end of the down platform now leaves by a single lead junction. The auto trailer is now a BR converted brake third and Stourbridge's 6434 has replaced 6418. Despatches from local manufacturers, in the form of two prams and a galvanised coal scuttle, await collection by the next up parcels service. 10 June 1964. *(Paul Burchill)*

210. The 5.40 pm Snow Hill-Stourbridge all stations local gets away from Old Hill station behind 6959 *Peatling Hall*. 13 April 1964. *(Paul Burchill)*

211. The 8.35 am Cardiff-Birmingham, consisting of a fine set of Great Western bow-ended coaches, climbs through the station at Cradley Heath & Cradley behind Hereford's 6989 *Wightwick Hall* in around 1954. The tracks in the foreground, alongside the wall of the Cradley Boiler Company, gave access to the short Corngreaves and Spinner's End (Old Hill Goods) branches. *(Keith Tilbrook)*

212. The platforms at Cradley were staggered, with a level crossing supervised by Cradley East Signal Box between them. 6926 *Holkham Hall* is seen departing from the down platform with the 5.5 pm Birmingham-Hartlebury. 10 May 1965. *(Paul Burchill)*

213. Cradley's yard lay on the up side, opposite the down platform. A local Bank train is pictured on 29 June 1966, with 9614 in charge. It will be noticed that the signal arm for the Corngreaves branch has been removed, the line having closed the previous year. *(Paul Burchill)*

214. An up passenger train, probably the 7.45 am Stourbridge Junction-Birmingham, approaches Lye behind 5379 of Worcester shed. c1955. *(Keith Tilbrook)*

215. An up Stourbridge-Birmingham, typically formed of non-corridor suburban stock and a 5101 tank, approaches Lye station. The sharp-eyed may make out the distant Stourbridge Engine Shed Signal Box on the West Midland line at the foot of the nearest telegraph pole. *(Keith Tilbrook)*

216. Shortly after passing Lye, the 12.45 pm Birmingham-Cardiff express in the hands of 6992 *Arborfield Hall* is seen in a typical Black Country industrial landscape at Timmis' Sidings, which served yet more fireclay and brick works. c1956. *(Keith Tilbrook)*

217. The 12.45 pm Snow Hill-Cardiff express is seen behind 6989 *Wightwick Hall*, a regular locomotive on these services at this time, around 1955. *(Keith Tilbrook)*

218. An up train of mineral empties makes its way north and approaches Timmis' Sidings with 6307 of Tyseley shed with a short train of wooden-bodied wagons that clearly falls short of that requiring banking assistance. *(Keith Tilbrook)*

Above: **219.** The Birmingham-Cardiff expresses were generally the preserve of locomotives from Tyseley and Hereford sheds, but a Sunday morning diagram brought a Canton 'Hall'. 4946 *Moseley Hall* approaches Stourbridge Junction with the return to the Welsh city. c1956. *(Keith Tilbrook)*

Opposite above: **220.** The 7.55 am Hereford-Birmingham express passes under Hungary Hill road bridge behind 5998 *Trevor Hall*, passing the branch home signals of Stourbridge Junction North Signal Box, for, from left to right, the No.2 Back Loop, the No.1 Loop and the Up Main respectively. The mileposts of the Stourbridge Extension line were from Paddington via Snow Hill, whereas those on the West Midland line were from Paddington via Oxford. Thus the train depicted would have been classified as a down train to Stourbridge North and an up train for the remainder of its journey. *(Keith Tilbrook)*

Opposite below: **221.** The hard work will begin shortly for Tyseley's 6904 *Charfield Hall* as it coasts round the curve on to the Stourbridge Extension line with an up express. With the load approaching the limit of 260 tons the eight coach train will tax the 'Hall' on the climb to Rowley Regis. *(Keith Tilbrook)*

222. The severe curve from the Extension to the main line at Stourbridge North is evident as the well-turned out 6971 *Athelhampton Hall*, in the prevailing BR mixed traffic black livery, sweeps under Hungary Hill bridge with the 9.45 am Birmingham Snow Hill-Cardiff express in around 1956. *(Keith Tilbrook)*

223. The finale of steam at Stourbridge really came with the closure of the engine shed in July 1966. The Western Region had determined that steam operations should cease at the end of 1965, so through steam-hauled trains were a rarity. One such is seen here as 92107 heads south past Stourbridge Junction North Signal Box with a train of welded rails from Hookagate, probably destined for the Permanent Way Depot at Newland, between Worcester and Malvern, on 30 June 1966. It is interesting to compare this photograph with the earlier one of 6950 at the same location, and note the signalling alterations that had been effected during the decade. *(Paul Dorney)*

224. How better to finish than with a final look at Stourbridge Junction in its 1950s heyday, with the 9.35 am Worcester-Crewe standing in the down main platform behind the celebrated 4079 *Pendennis Castle*, newly ex-works, returning to its home shed at Stafford Road Wolverhampton. The 'Town Car' is seen in Platform 1 with 1438, and a 5101 class tank busies itself by the South Box. 1954. *(Keith Tilbrook)*

BIBLIOGRAPHY

Cooke R. A., *Atlas of The Great Western Railway* (Wild Swan, 1988)

Jenkins S. C. & Quayle H. I., *The Oxford, Worcester & Wolverhampton Railway* (Oakwood, 1977)

Shill R., *Birmingham and the Black Country's Canalside Industries* (Tempus, 2005)

Hale M. and Williams N., *By Rail to Halesowen* (Michael Hale / Uralia Press, 1974)

Hale M., *Traffic and Transport in Nineteenth Century Kingswinford* (Woodsetton, 2000)

Butcher C., *The Railways of Stourbridge* (Oakwood Press, 1998)

Butcher C., *The GWR at Stourbridge and the Black Country* (Oakwood Press, 2004)

Collins P., *Rail Centres: Wolverhampton* (Ian Allan, 1990)

Christiansen R., *Regional History of the Railways of Great Britain, The West Midlands* (D&C,1973)

Beck K. M., *The West Midland Lines of the GWR* (Ian Allan, 1983)

INDEX OF LOCATIONS